A Divine Blessing

A Well–Kept Secret of Life's Second Half

A Divine Blessing

A Well-Kept Secret of Life's Second Half

Elizabeth Skoglund

World Wide Publications
A Ministry of the Billy Graham Evangelistic Association
1303 Hennepin Avenue, Minneapolis, Minnesota 55403

A Divine Blessing
A Well–Kept Secret of Life's Second Half

World Wide Publications is the publishing ministry of the Billy Graham Evangelistic Association.

Unless otherwise indicated, Scripture quotations are from the *King James Version* of the Bible.

Scripture quotations marked TLB are taken from *The Living Bible* and are used by permission, © 1971 by Tyndale House Publishing, Wheaton, IL.

Scripture quotations marked Weymouth are taken from *Weymouth's New Testament in Modern Speech* by Richard Francis Weymouth, as revised by J.A. Robertson. Published by special arrangement with James Clarke and Company Ltd., London. Reprinted by permission of Harper and Row Publishers, Inc. and James Clarke and Company Ltd.

Library of Congress Catalog Card Number:
88–50711

ISBN: 0–89066–109–X

Printed in the United States of America

Contents

(Where mention is made of people involved in professional counseling situations, names, gender and nonessential details have been altered to protect their privacy.)

DEDICATION

To Dorothy May Wittig Jones, who has exemplified through the years the words of the nineteenth–century poet Matthew Arnold, in his poem, "Rugby Chapel":

If, in the paths of the world,
Stones might have wounded thy feet,
Toil or dejection have tried
Thy spirit, of that we saw
Nothing—to us thou wast still
Cheerful, and helpful, and firm!
Therefore to thee it was given
Many to save with thyself;
And, at the end of thy day,
O faithful shepherd! to come
Bringing thy sheep in thy hand.

Chapter One

The Second Half

It was a chance meeting with an elderly lady on the sidewalk of a small town in the country. A friend and I had gone there to spend a summer afternoon, and the lady, like the two of us, appeared to be spending her time just looking at store windows.

We smiled, and she asked me about my dog Horace. We chatted a bit, but I don't even remember much that was said. Her looks, too, like the conversation, were not outstanding. She had ordinary white hair pulled back into a simple knot. Her clothes were plain but neat. Yet from her face emanated a glow and a look of contentment which distinguished her from other passers–by.

My day in this country town had been a small attempt to make up for vacation plans which had fallen through. I had been discouraged and weary. Yet somehow the cheeriness and inner joy of this stranger, whose name I never even knew, was contagious. I felt my own inner joy renewed. Then, just before we went our separate ways, she mentioned "her Lord." And I knew our meeting had been no chance meeting at all.

When my friend and I stopped for coffee later that afternoon, we got into a discussion about old age and our own prospects of aging. We shared our feelings of amazement at how fast life seemed to be moving for both of us. To me in particular, since my friend was younger, old age seemed a growing reality for the not–so–distant future. In place of the days of childhood and youth when one feels a sense of infinite strength and endless time, a sense of mortality was beginning to dawn on me. Someday I would be old. Someday I would die.

As we continued our conversation, I realized how much I wanted to be like the lady we had just met in the small country town. I wanted to be a reflection to others of the contentment and the encouragement of Jesus Christ. I wanted to be so made into his image, so refined by years of following him, that the transition from earth to heaven would not need to be such a dramatic change.

I was reminded, too, of the dear friend to whom this book is dedicated. I have known her since I was fifteen, meeting her first as the mother of schoolmates. I have known her through bad times as well as good times. She has been a source of comfort for me, a connection with my youth, a friend who knew members of my family who are now in heaven. A while back when she came to visit she was the first house guest in what was at that time my newly-decorated guest room. That night before we retired, we talked for a while—about the past, but also about the Lord. As she talked I watched her face and was impressed with the depth of contentment and love I saw there. I believe that when the Lord takes her home his refining process will be as close to being completed as it can be on this earth. That's what I want to be like at her age.

> . . . But all of us, as with unveiled faces we mirror the glory of the Lord, are transformed into the same likeness, from glory to glory, even as derived from the Lord the Spirit (2 Cor. 3:18 Weymouth).

In his commentary on 2 Corinthians, Bishop H. C. G. Moule translates this verse:

> We reflect as a mirror the glory of the Lord Christ on our brow, we are transforming in that blessed sunshine into the same image, from glory to glory, from stage to stage of likeness to Himself, . . . [1]

This transforming process should be the Christian's goal in aging.

An Honor, Not a Curse

Contrary to popular thinking, God never meant old age to be a curse. Nor was the physical process of aging meant to be hidden out of embarrassment by the excessive use of cosmetics or cosmetic surgery. To be old was not meant to be a cause of shame; rather, the Bible presents old age as a state to be desired for oneself and honored by others. Indeed, the only one of the Ten Commandments connected with a promise offers long life as the incentive.

When I was a student in graduate school I lived with a Chinese family whose home served as the United States headquarters for a missionary work in Hong Kong and Taiwan. The unspoken head of the "family" of missionaries living there was always designated by age. When the oldest missionary had her birthday, for example, it was a truly grand affair compared to that of any of us who were younger. Our birthdays were happy times, but for those who were older the celebrations became increasingly elaborate in order to celebrate the achievement of age. Age was respected and desired, but it was not worshiped.

In a way which helped me clarify the balance between too much emphasis on length of life and too little emphasis, I once heard William F. Buckley, Jr., state something to the effect that, while a love of life is healthy, a veneration of age is idolatry. Consistent with that thought, he observed that Christ would not have died on the cross if he had venerated life. I thought his point was well taken. When the Bible speaks of age as a blessing and even a reward it encourages a love of life, not its worship. An idolatry of life can cripple a person. Long life in itself, regardless of its meaning, becomes the goal. Risk is eliminated at any cost.

Aging can be an achievement. That's why it is so sad to go through a department store and see older ladies who have had plastic surgery so many times that their faces are no longer their own. They look like plastic dolls. I can certainly understand plastic surgery for disfigurement caused by accident or burns or by birth defects. I can even understand its value for people when aging is unusually accentuated in some way. But wrinkles in the face and furrows on the brow can be distinguishing signs of wisdom, to be honored in those who have endured and grown and contributed with their lives, and who now have a distilled reservoir of knowledge to offer those who are still young.

The argument might well be raised that age does not necessarily bring wisdom, that the elderly are not always wise or godly. Yet perhaps the reason why some older people just give up has something to do with how younger people treat them. For so long now we have expected senility in old age and have viewed the advancing years as a liability that we have, in part, produced that result. The German philosopher Goethe once observed that, if we treat people as they are, we help them to stay as they are; but if we treat them as if they were already what they were capable of becoming, then we help them to realize that potential. Goethe's words ring especially true with regard to how we treat the aged. Our expectations of ourselves and others have a great deal to do with what we all become.

A century ago the English poet Robert Browning wrote of age from a perspective very different from that of our day. Indeed his words may sound unrealistic to us, even ridiculous, when at the age of fifty-two, perhaps dealing with his own aging process, Browning wrote:

> Grow old along with me!
> The best is yet to be,
> The last of life, for which the first was
>   made:
> Our times are in His hand
> Who saith "A whole I planned,
> Youth shows but half; trust God: see all
>   nor be afraid!" 2

Yet today even more than in Browning's day, the second half of life can be a period of reaping the good one has sown. And it can also be a time of great productivity. Due to advances in medical technology our chances for long life are greater now than they were for our grandparents or even our parents. It is perhaps an irony characteristic of the human race that while we have spent our history looking for the so-called fountain of youth, now that our life expectancy has increased we don't always know what to do with those extra years. In some cases we even seek a justification for terminating life now that it has been extended.

Second Half or Third Quarter?

We have been talking about life's "second half." But the increase in life expectancy has caused some experts to refer to the period of life between fifty and seventy-five as the "third quarter" of life, and to view it as a time of peak productivity. In *Our Aging Society*, Alan Pifer and Lydia Bronte say, "Since 1900—less than a century ago—our life expectancy has increased by twenty-eight years, from forty-seven to seventy-five." [3] (From that measurement of life expectancy, Robert Browning had already outlived his life expectancy by five years at the time he wrote so optimistically about old age!) Pifer and Bronte continue:

> Age sixty–five has become obsolete as a basis for life–course policy. A more realistic basis for policy might be a new concept we call the "third quarter of life," the years from about fifty to about seventy–five—the lower age selected because it is a time of change for many people, and the upper because it is only after age sev-

enty–five that many people begin to decline physically and mentally. Since the majority of Americans at the age of fifty today still have a third to a half of their life spans ahead of them, and since people between the ages of fifty and seventy–five will soon constitute nearly a third of the population, the third–quarter concept assumes that one's fifties and early sixties need not and should not be a period of gradual withdrawal and decline toward an inevitable cut–off point of age sixty–five. 4

Today more than ever there is the chance for "the last of life" to be a time of a special blending of wisdom and learning, combined with enough physical strength to make a concrete contribution to the world.

Whatever old age becomes to each of us, however, depends on our own attitudes. If we determine that our aging is going to be a downhill process, it probably will be just that. If we decide it can be a positive time, there is a good chance that it will be.

Anthropologist Colin Turnbull, in his remarkable book, *The Mountain People*, writes about the Ik tribe of Uganda, who have a very low regard for anyone who is physically limited due to old age or any other cause. Formerly hunters, the Ik were forced by changing circumstances to give up hunting and to seek survival by farming, in an area too infertile for agriculture. From that time on the tribe deteriorated until they are now nearly extinct. The Ik, Turnbull found, have given up trying; they seem almost completely devoid of even basic emotions such as grief. The Ik provide a graphic example of man's inhumanity to man apart from God. They abandon the very young and the very old. Parents throw their children out to fend for themselves. Children steal food out of the mouths of their own dying parents. Old people are laughed at when they fall and they are left to starve to death. Government relief is mismanaged, causing some to grow fat while others go hungry. Says Turnbull, "There is no goodness left for the Ik, only a full stomach, and that only for those whose stomachs are already full." [5]

Turnbull applies what has happened to the Ik to changes in our own culture:

> What has become of the Western family? The very old and the very young are separated, but we dispose of them in homes for the aged or in day schools and summer camps. . . . [6]

And he concludes, in words which from a human point of view are filled with frightening implications:

> The Ik teach us that our much vaunted human values are not inherent in humanity at all, but are associated only with a particular form of survival called society, and that all, even society itself, are luxuries that can be dispensed with. That does not make them any the less wonderful or desirable, and if man has any greatness it is surely in his ability to maintain these values, clinging to them to an often very bitter end, even shortening an already pitifully

short life rather than sacrificing his humanity.
But that too involves choice, and the Ik teach us
that man can lose the will to make it. 7

"White Hair Is a Crown of Glory"

God's view of human life in general, and
aging in particular, is very different from
that of the Ik, or of those who would depend
only on cultural norms to determine the
value of the elderly. As God sees it, old age
is not just a time of potential productivity; it
is also a time of reward and glory. Our Lord
would surely agree with the words of
Browning that "the best is yet to be."

In Leviticus 19:32 we read the command,
"Thou shalt rise up before the hoary head,
and honour the face of the old man. . . ."
Proverbs 16:31 (TLB) says, "White hair is a
crown of glory and is seen most among the
godly." Consistent with the attitude that
old age is to be respected, we read in Proverbs 20:29 (TLB), "The glory of young men is
their strength; of old men, their experience." And in Job 5:26 we see that old age is
most certainly a reward of the Lord: "Thou
shalt come to thy grave in a full age, like as a
shock of corn cometh in his season."

The apostle Paul also speaks of the qualities that should characterize old age:

> . . . that the aged men be sober, grave, temper-
> ate, sound in faith, in charity, in patience. The
> aged women likewise, that they be in behaviour
> as becometh holiness, not false accusers, not

given to much wine, teachers of good things; that they may teach the young women to be sober, to love their husbands, to love their children, to be discreet, chaste, keepers at home, good, obedient to their own husbands, that the word of God be not blasphemed (Titus 2:2–5).

Paul's standards reflect the ideal which God holds out for old age. But the choice must still be made to become that ideal. It is not automatic.

Long after the death of my aunt Ruth, who was a missionary in China, I was going through the pages of one of her books and discovered a clipping on aging which she had pasted inside the front cover. It reads:

Famed war correspondent Col. Frederick Palmer called on General Douglas MacArthur at his Manila headquarters. His most vivid memory: three frames over the general's desk. One, a portrait of Washington; one, a portrait of Lincoln; one, the framed message which you will read in part below. The general has had it in sight ever since it was given to him by John W. Lewis, Jr., in April of 1942, when he was fighting 2,000 miles from Manila:

"Youth is not a time of life—it is a state of mind.

"Nobody grows old by merely living a number of years; people grow old only by deserting their ideals. Years may wrinkle the skin, but to give up interest wrinkles the soul. Worry, doubt, self-distrust, fear and despair—these are the long, long years that bow the head and turn the growing spirit back to dust.

"Whether seventy or sixteen, there is in every being's heart the love of wonder, the sweet amazement at the stars and the starlike things and thoughts, the undaunted challenge of events, the unfailing childlike appetite for what next, and then joy and the game of life.

"You are as young as your faith, as old as your doubt; as young as your hope, as old as your despair."

—Samuel Ullman

In his biography of the man who may well have been the greatest general this country has ever produced, William Manchester adds words from MacArthur which, combined with the above, offer a good definition of old age:

In the central place of every heart there is a recording chamber; so long as it receives messages of beauty, hope, cheer and courage, so long are you young. When . . . your heart is covered with the snows of pessimism and the ice of cynicism, then and then only are you grown old—and then, indeed, as the ballad says, you just fade away. 8

The apostle Paul expresses a similar truth in Philippians 4:8:

Finally, brethren, whatsoever things are true, whatsoever things are honest, whatsoever things are just, whatsoever things are pure, whatsoever things are lovely, whatsoever things are of good report; if there be any virtue, and if there be any praise, think on these things.

One of the surest ways to avoid the debilitating potential of old age is to saturate oneself in the positiveness of the Word of God.

We cannot change the attitudes of a nation overnight. But we can change our own attitude. How we view old age as individuals will make all the difference regarding how we treat the aged and how we handle our own aging. Growing old in America in the late twentieth century is not always an experience to be looked forward to. But that doesn't have to be the case for us as individuals.

When I was growing up, my best friends in the neighborhood had their grandparents living with them. The grandparents made themselves useful by their babysitting services, by smoking meat in the outside "garden house," and by helping to build on an extra bedroom, among other things. For their grandchildren they provided endless joy, a joy which reached its apex for all of us neighborhood children when the grandfather hand-carved a beautiful, life-sized rocking horse with a real tail!

Not long ago I came across a diary which I had written at about age ten. In it I proudly commented that my friends' grandparents had given me a rabbit. Not too important from an adult point of view, but to a child it provided a lifelong memory of happiness. And because I had never known my own grandparents, these people provided just a little of the joy I had missed. More importantly, they helped me see old age more as a time of fulfillment than of disability and hopelessness. They helped to shape my own developing view of aging.

Chapter Two

Choosing Your Way

J im and I last saw each other when we were in grade school. We both played violin in the school orchestra, and his sister Sonja and I were best friends in sixth grade. After that we all changed schools, and Jim and Sonja moved to another state. Except for an occasional Christmas card through the years, we lost all contact with each other.

Then last summer, some forty years later, Jim called me "out of the blue" to tell me that Sonja had died that spring after a long battle with cancer. Jim explained that both Sonja and he had expected to die of heart attacks after both of their parents died that way, and that the cancer had been a surprise. He went on to tell of other classmates who had lost children, of some who had died, and of one who was already in a convalescent home because she had a progressive muscular disease. He talked a little about his career in law, a career which he had eventually given up because he had "no feel for it," a career which he had only taken up in the first place because of his father's prodding. In a final burst of what had been an escalating output of gloom, Jim concluded, "Maybe my productive days are over. What I do with the rest of my life won't really make any long-term difference anyway! After all, Elizabeth, you have to remember, we're getting old!"

As I placed the telephone receiver slowly down I took a deep breath and looked out the bedroom window at the trees across the street and the mountains in the distance. The world outside looked the same. I hadn't aged a day. But I felt thirty years older! Jim had made a choice to live in his gloomy thoughts and to share them whenever possible. He had made a choice to be old in the worst possible sense of that word.

In contrast, I remembered a few years ago when my aunt Lydia had broken her hip for the third time. She was eighty-eight years old; x-rays showed that her hip bones were literally paper-thin from extreme osteoporosis. After performing some complicated surgery designed uniquely for her nearly inoperable bones, the surgeon told me that my aunt would never walk again.

"Are you saying that she can't physically put her weight on her bones," I asked, "or are you assuming that, after three hip fractures and a serious car accident, she'll choose to give up?"

"The latter," he replied slowly. "I just don't see how anyone that age can go through all that and still learn to walk again."

My aunt had a choice: to put all of her energies into walking again, or to give up. She chose to walk, and that decision made all the difference in what was to be the last year of her life on this earth.

Choice is a major key to aging gracefully. Choice gives us alternatives and freedom. Choice grants a sense of independence. Yet one of the popular myths of aging is that somehow age destroys the power of choice.

A lady in her late sixties once visited my counseling office. I had always heard from my colleagues how difficult it was to effectively counsel the elderly. "They just don't change," was the general consensus of opinion, "or if they do, it takes a very long time." In essence, they no longer have freedom of choice. At the time this particular lady sought my help, I had just began my counseling career and therefore was not unaffected by my colleagues' opinions. I had never treated an older person, and this lady was sure she was beyond hope to start with! The combination of attitudes did not get us off to a good start.

However, there has always been a side to my personality which has resisted categorizing people. When I taught school, for example, I rarely checked a student's record to see how smart he was or what his behavior was like, until I had had a chance to get to know him on my own. Such an approach gave the student a fresh chance; and I decided to try to help my first elderly patient with that same positive attitude.

The results were positive—and more quickly achieved than in some of my younger patients. The lady stopped giving her things away and began inviting her friends to her house again. She resumed her gardening and church-going. She began driving her car; she started to think of helping other older people, almost as if she were the young person and they were the elderly ones. It wasn't that she played a game about her age; she actually felt younger because she had chosen to act according to her capacity, not according to what she thought she should feel at her age.

The Bible emphasizes choice—both the choice of God toward man and the choice of man toward God. "Choose you this day whom ye will serve. . ." (Joshua 24:15) is God's command to us as well as to ancient Israel. John 15:16 presents the balance of God's choice regarding us: "Ye have not chosen me, but I have chosen you. . . ." There is man's choice and God's choice — paradoxical but not intrinsically contradictory. For there is a certain "unknowableness" about God which is in itself a proof of his reality. God by definition must be somewhat incomprehensible to finite man or he would cease to be God.

When Paul urges us to "present all your faculties" for God's service (see Weymouth's translation of Romans 12:1, 2), he is speaking of a choice which God demands regardless of our age. He doesn't accept the excuse that our faculties are fading and are therefore not worthy of presenting to him. Indeed they are a "sacrifice acceptable to him," and as such are to be considered of great value by us. We are commanded to choose God's view of us— and his view is that each of us has inestimable worth. When we choose God's viewpoint, it will be impossible to consider our time of old age as time wasted. We will not throw away the productivity of those years.

Choosing Our Thoughts

One of the areas of greatest difficulty regarding choice is controlling our thoughts. As noted in the preceding chapter, all of us, at every age, carry around in our minds "tape recordings" of memories from the past and fears of the future. And if the contents of these mental "tapes" are not controlled, they can easily get out of hand.

With so much in the news today about child abuse, for example, many people who are well on in life are beginning to dredge up memories of past acts of abuse from their childhood. Sometimes the memories are of real acts of abuse, but at other times the recollections are exaggerated by the passage of time or are even non-existent, fostered, perhaps, by an over-enthusiastic friend or even a counselor who feels that "something just must have happened if you feel this way." These people may have been perfectly happy with their lives until they "remembered" some childhood act of violence against them. Then the tapes start to play. "Didn't my parents love me?" "Was I a bad person to let it happen?" "Why didn't my mother protect me?" Experiences which have been dealt with long ago, or which may not have even happened, are thought about until they feel as though they have just occurred all over again.

Memories can torment people as they grow older and begin to review their lives. There are regrets about that career which was neglected or never started. Some feel guilt over how their children have turned out. The list of possible regrets is endless, and they can easily turn into old tapes which so torment us by the past that they diminish our effectiveness for the present and the future.

During the fortieth anniversary year of the deliverance of Hitler's notorious death camp, Auschwitz, many survivors made a pilgrimage back to the camp. Many of them found that, although they had felt that the forty years had healed the worst of their memories of Auschwitz, when they returned for the anniversary those memories came flooding back. They remembered. The pain and reality of this earthly pit of hell came back as if it had just happened. The tapes of memory had not been erased; they had just been turned off for forty years.

The effects of playing old tapes from the past can range from mild discomfort to total despair and self-destruction. Joseph, who had endured two years in Hitler's death camps, came to the United States and developed a profitable business as a goldsmith. The death camp memories were never eradicated, but they were under control. He had a focus—his work and his family. Only rarely did Joseph allow himself the "luxury" of playing the tapes of those terrible years, and then only to a limited degree.

As Joseph moved toward retirement his family and friends urged him to slow down, to retire and turn his business over to his son. They meant well and no one could have foreseen what the tragic results would be. Not long after Joseph's retirement, he began to talk more about the camps again. Well-meaning friends thought that perhaps this was good. Maybe Joseph had needed to get this all out of his system for a long time, they reasoned. But eventually he became moody and withdrawn. He no longer talked much. He just thought—and remembered!

Today, in his mind, Joseph is back in Auschwitz with the barbed wire and the cruelty of the SS. He is making jewelry again, but not for the public. He is plying his trade as he did in 1944—to please the Gestapo and thus to stay alive. Because the tapes went out of control, Joseph now lives in the reality of those tapes. To him the horrors of the death camps are happening all over again. Joseph is insane.

Most of us do not play the negative tapes of the past to the degree that they totally take over our lives. But particularly for the elderly, even a seemingly limited amount of tape-playing can bring gloom to an otherwise happy life. *Choice* is the key to how much this happens to any of us.

Old age is a time many of us fear because we have preconceived ideas about what it will be like. We play tapes of the *future* as well as of the past. Old age may be feared as a time when all choice is removed and others make our decisions for us. Broken hips, convalescent homes, loneliness, poverty, senility: sometimes these are a tangible part of aging, and when they occur they increase our feeling of helplessness. But many older people never actually experience these things; they are just the "what-if's" which torture almost as much as the real thing. Or if they do actually occur, they may compose only a small part of the whole time of being old.

The fear of Alzheimer's is a good example of this fear of the future. Any real memory loss should certainly be checked out by a physician. But a great many elderly people suffer needless torture by questioning themselves every time they forget anything. Just the other day a middle-aged lady who came for her appointment at the wrong time said in a state of near panic, "What if I'm getting Alzheimer's? I seem to be so forgetful." Yet I have teenagers who come at the wrong time more than once and never doubt their sanity at all.

While the destructive potential of playing mental tapes is obvious, these tapes shouldn't be confused with genuine feelings. We in California are prone to experiencing earthquakes. If the quake is strong enough to move the foundations under our feet, and at the same time we hear glass clashing, we are going to experience fear. For a while after the earth stops shaking, we shake. We talk, we express concern, and we worry about the next one.

After a while, however, the fear diminishes. The quake is over, the after-shocks become less frequent, and life settles back into normal as the earth beneath us does the same. We go on. Yet after a sizeable quake there are always a few people who think about the "what-if's" and wonder when "the big one" will hit. Such thoughts are examples of the mental tapes we've been talking about. The only solution to such tape-playing is to make a choice to cut them off, and to focus on something positive and absorbing.

A few nights after the last quake, I was lying in my bed thinking about whether or not a quake or an after-shock would awaken me. As my anxiety grew I realized with a jolt what I was doing. I was beginning to play and replay a tape which had the potential to destroy my night's sleep. I resolutely cut the tape off. Then because I find such books absorbing, I picked up an Agatha Christie mystery and began to read. Soon the mystery became more real to me than my tape about earthquakes, and I was sound asleep.

Evening in Paris

To age gracefully it is important to control the old, negative tapes. They must be cut off in one's mind and the focus must be put somewhere else. Yet it is of equal importance to recognize, and to utilize, those tapes which are *positive*. Memories of the past which encourage, as long as they don't turn into regrets, can be a heritage of old age. Remembering how adorable little Suzy was at her first birthday party can be rewarding as long as that tape doesn't become a regret that Suzy is not all she could be as an adult.

Old photo albums, mementos, cherished gifts from those who have gone on to be with the Lord, letters, pieces of music, favorite recipes which we used to associate with a pleasant holiday time: such memories can be a comfort in old age. The key to their success in helping rather than hindering is to choose to keep them as positive tapes, not negative ones. Right after the death of a spouse, a cherished letter which was written way back in the days of courtship might only aggravate the fresh wounds of grief. Two years later, when there has been greater emotional healing, the letter might be enjoyable and comforting. It would then provide a positive tape of the past.

One does not have to be very old to derive pleasure and comfort from treasured mementos. Teenagers keep childhood teddy bears, even though they may be ragged and worn. The idea that a bride should wear something old, as well as something new, is another example of this need for reminders of the past.

When I was about four years old I would sometimes go with my father to the corner drug store. I have no idea what he bought because each time I became absorbed at the cosmetic counter looking longingly at clear, cobalt blue bottles of perfume. They were to me the epitome of beauty. I later learned the perfume was called "Evening in Paris." I deeply wanted to own a bottle. Obviously at four years of age no one took me seriously. And then the perfume disappeared from the marketplace.

Last summer, some forty years later, I walked into a department store and there they were, those beautiful, cobalt blue bottles of perfume. Trying not to show my childish excitement I asked the clerk about them. Yes, she told me, these bottles were made from the same molds as the old "Evening in Paris." It was the same perfume, now renamed. But best of all, these were the same bottles which I had admired as a child. As I bought my bottle, I didn't care what the perfume smelled like or how much it cost. It was for me simply a memento, a positive tape from a period of life full of good memories. The clerk told me that "Evening in Paris" had been taken off of the market at the time of the devastation of France during World War II. For many that period of history was not a happy one. But for me at age four it had been a time of security in a family that loved me; and that blue bottle had become a happy reminder of those days.

Choosing Our Attitudes

Sometimes, of course, even when one's choices are positive and the mental tapes are under control, the worst fears of old age become reality. All the planning in the world doesn't eliminate them. Yet even when the "what-if's" become a real part of our old age, we can still choose our attitude toward them.

Speaking of the meaning which can be discovered even when life is "neither fruitful in creation nor rich in experience," psychiatrist Dr. Viktor Frankl explains:

> His very response to the restraints upon his potentialities provides him with a new realm of values which surely belong among the highest values. Thus an apparently impoverished existence—one which is poor in creative and experiential values—still offers a last, and in fact the greatest, opportunity for the realization of values. These values we will call attitudinal values. What is significant is the person's attitude toward an unalterable fate. 1

Frankl concludes, "A man's life retains its meaning up to the last—until he draws his last breath." 2

Drawing from his understanding of suffering which he developed in the concentration camps of World War II, Dr. Frankl gives a touching example of meaning in the middle of suffering. Quoting the words of another camp inmate, Frankl says:

> All of us in camp, my comrades and myself as well, were certain that no happiness on earth could ever in the future make up for what we were compelled to endure during our imprisonment. If we had drawn up a balance sheet of happiness, the only choice left to us would have been to "run into the wire"—that is, to kill ourselves. Those who did not do so were acting out of a deep sense of some obligation. As far as I was concerned, I felt duty-bound toward my mother to stay alive. We two loved one another

beyond all else. Therefore my life had a meaning—in spite of everything. 3

The choice to find meaning is the obligation laid upon us in the middle of any un-
avoidable suffering, whether that suffering
is thrust upon us in old age or whether it
happens to us earlier in life. It is, indeed,
the ultimate of choices.

Missionary Amy Carmichael had always
dreaded the thought of having a lingering
illness which would inconvenience those
around her. Her desire was that when she
died she would go quickly. Yet before her
Lord took her to himself, she endured years
of illness. The body gave out before the
mind and the spirit. Her greatest fear of old
age came true. Yet out of those years and
that illness came *Rose From Brier*, a book
written from the ill to the ill, a book which
has helped untold numbers of people in
bearing their suffering. Amy Carmichael
chose her attitude toward her suffering;
she chose not to waste it.

Old at Sixteen; Young at Eighty

When my dog Thackeray died last summer I missed him greatly. He was an utterly
devoted dog; my new dog Horace had a
great deal to live up to. As you might sus-
pect, Horace quickly wound his way into
my heart. However, Horace has a major social problem. He barks. Like Thackeray, he

is a sheltie. But he is a small sheltie instead of a big one, and so his bark, in addition to being frequent, is also high and squeaky. At first I thought, "This is ridiculous. People come to me with their emotional problems and they get help. I can certainly cure a dog of barking." Then just yesterday, I finally gave up and called a dog trainer, only to hear the trainer decisively declare, "He's just too old. You should have done this when he was young." Now, Horace is ten *months* old—not even seven years old by human standards. Yet to this trainer he's old! Needless to say, I chose a different trainer—one who thinks Horace is still young.

There is something rather relative about age which makes its definition more dependent than we realize upon our choice of attitude. I'd never thought of fifty-five as old age until I saw a rather defensive bumper sticker the other day. It read, "Over 55 and loving it." Apparently someone thinks fifty-five marks the onset of old age.

That "Over 55" bumper sticker reminded me of all the high school students I taught years ago who were already set and "old." I learned then that it was possible to be old at sixteen. But most of all it made me think of all the elderly people I know who are *young.* My mother was eighty when she was killed in a car accident, but she was young. She did oil paintings, baked delicious pies,

cakes and cookies, took care of her own
yard, and was always ready to go out on the
spur of the moment. She had her infirmities, among them severe arthritis which
would have relegated many people to a
wheelchair. But she chose a positive attitude toward her age and disability.

What we choose to become in old age is a
challenge, not only for our own comfort but
for the inspiration of those around us and
even of the unseen world. In Hebrews 12:1
we are told that we are surrounded by heavenly witnesses who, I believe, are a sort of
cheering section for those of us who still
serve our Lord on this earth. Consistent with this thought, according to
Weymouth's translation of 1 Corinthians
11:10, angels are spectators of human activity. Bible scholar F. L. Godet further
supports this interpretation:

> According to Luke 15:7,10, the angels in
> heaven hail the conversion of every sinner; . . .
> according to Ephesians 3:10, they behold with
> adoration the infinitely diversified wonders
> which the Divine Spirit works within the
> Church: . . . according to 1 Timothy 5:21, they
> are, as well as God and Jesus Christ, witnesses
> of the ministry of Christ's servants; . . . 4

Conceivably, then, we encourage the unseen world as well as ourselves and those
around us by our choices. This thought in
itself should be a tremendous motivating
factor; but above all, we know that God

himself is the ultimate One whom we wish to please.

Old age is an achievement. We can't help what we are born with, but we can decide what we will become. At no period of life is that choice filled with more challenge than in the years of old age—years which sometimes bring with them infirmities and limitations, and which are so often viewed by society as years of waste and even degradation. Yet if we act with self-respect in the years of old age, we will gain the respect of those around us. We will truly choose our own way.

Chapter Three

The Safety Zones of Aging

T he last time I ever saw my uncle Dave he was lying very still in his hospital bed. He was in his nineties and had been ill for several weeks. Illness was a new experience for him. Brought up on a farm in Wisconsin, he had eventually bought his own small farm; he had always worked hard and enjoyed the best of health. As the only son in a family of five girls he had taken on a man's workload early in life. Yet in contrast to this proof of his manliness, my first memory of Uncle Dave is of his sensitivity to me as a child when he taught me to play tennis and took me fishing on Lake Michigan.

Now as Uncle Dave lay in that bed he seemed to sense his vulnerability. We talked a little, mainly about the Lord; and then he turned his head toward me and looked at me intently. "When I get better I can come home, you know. I have enough money put aside to get outside help until I'm better." Then, reassured by his own declaration, he fell asleep. I was never to see him alive again.

During his life my uncle had worked hard and had always put money aside. His financial nest egg became in his old age a "safety zone," an anchor, which insured that he would maintain his independence for as long as possible. He never had to use it, and if a really major medical crisis had arisen it would not have been enough to pay the expenses. But that nest egg had been there throughout his old age. Its presence was worth more as an emotional safety zone than for what it could actually buy.

A safety zone is something into which we retreat temporarily from the stress of life. Safety zones can be simple, like a hot cup of tea on a chilly afternoon or the solitude of one's own place after a day in the crowds of the city. A book, a favorite restaurant, a chat with a friend, a drive in the country, a faithful dog, a photograph album: these are just a few of the many safety zones which all of us have and use, whether we realize it or not. They buffer us from the harshness of life; they absorb some of the pain of change.

During World War II there were places called "safe houses" which were used by the underground to hide people from the

Gestapo. In Budapest, when Adolph Eichmann was determined to eradicate the last large group of Jews in Europe, a young Swedish diplomat, Raoul Wallenberg, managed to set aside several such safe houses, where he could protect Jews from the Gestapo as well as the Arrowcross (the Hungarian Nazis). These safe houses were safety zones in the most concrete meaning of that term. They literally insured physical safety; in a period of nine months up to 100,000 Jews were saved from deportation to Hitler's death camps. Like the physical protection of these safe houses, emotional safety zones are important to the aging process. They help provide feelings of emotional and spiritual safety and well being.

In the old movie, "I Remember Mama," which tells the story of a Norwegian family in San Francisco, Mama starts talking about "the family bank account" whenever there's a crisis. She and Papa always tell the children that, if they have to, they can always go to the bank. But they never do go to the bank. There is always enough without that. At the end of the movie it turns out that there never was an account at the bank. But as Mama explained, children should not be brought up in insecurity. They must think there is something to fall back on. There must be a safety zone.

Old age, like childhood, can be threatened by dependence and vulnerability. Physical needs can multiply while a per-

son's ability to earn is diminishing. Yet un-
like childhood, when there are usually
many people available to tend to one's
needs, by the time a person reaches old age
family and friends may have moved far
away. Some will have died. Others, while
living nearby, may be in poor health. If ever
there is a time when one needs safety
zones, it is during old age. And perhaps one
of the more fundamental needs is the need
for a sense of financial security.

As I write those words I hesitate, because
it sounds so crass to emphasize financial
needs, when the needs of the mind and
spirit are so much more important. Yet too
often we ignore bodily and material needs
in our emphasis on the spiritual. Jesus did
not consider it beneath him to feed the mul-
titudes or to heal the sick. Our Lord could
be very practical, and we, his children, do
not need to feel guilty if we build the safety
zone of financial security into our prepara-
tions for old age.

As with so many issues, it is important to
maintain a balance in our attitude toward
money. Money cannot buy happiness.
Furthermore, as with my uncle, that seem-
ing fortune which we set aside will usually
be limited. Inflation and rising medical
costs will probably have a way of making
our nest egg less secure than we had
hoped. And, ultimately, God is above our
need for money. For he who notes the fall of
a sparrow and takes time to clothe a field of

flowers will not fail to keep in touch with the needs of those whom he loved enough to sacrifice his own Son. Yet balance is a principle of the Scriptures. And it is important, when possible, to take appropriate care in the establishment of a financial safety zone for our old age.

The Safety Zone of Dignity

Safety zones, however, refer to more than bank accounts. Dignity is a far more important safety zone of aging. We cannot reform overnight the view of a society which denigrates old age, but we can certainly deal with our own view of aging. Once again, we can choose our own way. To keep up on current events, to care about one's looks and the appearance of one's house, to keep on sending Christmas cards, to contribute to the needs of others—these are all indications of a person who considers himself to still be of importance to the world. A manicure or a regular haircut can be a safety zone; so can making cookies or buying a canary or chopping wood. Each activity provides a safety zone of dignity.

A woman in her late seventies who lost her last close relative said to me, "Don't let me neglect putting up my Christmas tree this year. I need to know that I'm going on." At the time her relative died she had allowed a friend to stay with her for a few days, but then graciously thanked the friend and told her she would be all right alone. While the companionship of a permanent house guest can be helpful for some in this situation, for this woman getting back to normal was a way of taking hold of the safety zone of dignity. She felt good about the way she had handled things, and that feeling of dignity helped her go on.

Finding the safety zone of dignity involves taking oneself seriously. Sometimes elderly people start giving things away, as if they had decided to stop living before they die. But life should be considered meaningful right up to the day of death. God has numbered our days, and he does not take even one of them lightly. Each one has meaning and purpose. To see this is to find the safety zone of dignity.

It was the spring of the year in which my mother was to die so abruptly. She and I had spent the day together at the ocean. After a late lunch we came home, driving slowly through an attractive residential area. Simultaneously we saw the estate sale sign and decided to "just take a look." The sale was a particularly good one and the articles being sold were unusual. My mother bought me a sconce, which I've had on my wall ever since. For me it provides a safety zone of memory—the memory of a happy day with my mother.

More important, however, the day at the estate sale provided a safety zone of dignity for my mother. After my father's death a few years earlier, my mother had kept living in the family house, had done the gardening, continued her home baking and, in general, had kept going on. That going on was, for her, a safety zone of dignity. But it was difficult, too, for increasingly she had become afflicted with arthritis. That day at the estate sale she even had a hard time walking up the slight incline which led to the house. But she was determined to go on. Once inside she spotted a small white writing desk bordered in gold trim. Her immediate impulse was to buy it, for it was something she had always wanted. Then suddenly she turned to me and asked, "Do you think I'd be foolish to buy this at my age?"

Through all eternity I'll be thankful for my answer of reassurance. For even though she died just four months later, she enjoyed her writing desk more in those four months than most people would have in a lifetime. And most importantly, it provided a safety zone of dignity. She was worth a new desk, for however long she would be here to use it. Her life still had value and as such was to be taken seriously.

The elderly people I know who live fulfilled lives do not live as though they were going to die tomorrow. They plan. They make out wills. They are not foolish or unrealistic about life, but they are wise enough to know that life at any age is uncertain.   Newborn infants die; teenagers die; no one has a guarantee on length of life. The happy, fulfilled elderly people I know are not defensive about their aging.   They are neither apologetic every time they forget something nor hesitant about commitments for the future, as though they might not be around to keep those commitments. They take their lives seriously and go on. They know the safety zone of dignity.

Memories and Meaning

Another source of great contentment as we grow older lies in the familiar, the old, the cherished. Certain places and objects act as reminders to us of the rich content our lives have held. They remind us of past pleasures and of those we have loved. They provide positive tapes, which in turn become safety zones. Above all, they remind us of the *meaning* which our lives have known. Too many people immediately sell their house and get rid of their belongings after the death of a spouse. Or even without a death, they get discouraged on just an ordinary day and decide they "have too much to keep up with." So they start to eliminate things which feel momentarily overwhelming. In the emotion of the moment they fail to discriminate between ordinary clutter and things which still comfort and hold meaning from the past—things which could still be safety zones. For the past in each of our lives is not dead; it is alive with meaning.

In his book, *The Unheard Cry for Meaning*, Viktor Frankl says:

> The pessimist resembles a man who observes with fear and sadness that his wall calendar, from which he daily tears a sheet, grows thinner with each passing day. On the other hand, the person who attacks the problems of life actively is like a man who removes each successive leaf from his calendar and files it neatly and carefully away with its predecessors, after first having jotted down a few diary notes on the back. He can reflect with pride and joy on all the richness set down in these notes, on all the life he has already lived to the full. What will it matter to him if he notices that he is growing old? Has he any reason to envy the young people he sees, or wax nostalgic over his own lost youth? What reasons has he to envy a young person? For the possibilities open to a young person, the future that is in store for him? "No, thank you," he will think. "Instead of possibilities, I have realities in my past, not only the reality of work done and of love loved, but of sufferings bravely suffered. These sufferings are the things of which I am most proud, though these are things which cannot inspire envy." [1]

While it is unhealthy to live in the past as though there were no present and no future, it is reckless to cast away all reminders of the past. For while the present is just happening and as such is uncertain, and the future is not guaranteed, as we get older our storehouse of achievement from the past becomes increasingly rich. It is the heritage of our life. It is a safety zone.

For some, of course, their achievements do not seem enough to count for a lifetime. Perhaps they underestimate what they have really done. For it is not just those who do great things in the eyes of the world whom God values. Sometimes he values more the widow's mite. God puts great emphasis on worship, prayer, and the good deeds which are done silently, outside of the vision and praise of man. He puts great value on suffering endured for him and on trust in him which was exercised when there was no explanation or reason given.

Still, there are those for whom life has been seemingly wasted. The first half of life has been used up on trivia and the second half does not seem to be yielding any greater value than the first. But for those who know Christ there comes the potential for meaning even in the latter days. For them the words in Joel 2:25,26 ring out with hope for yet finding the safety zone of meaning:

> And I will restore to you the years that the locust hath eaten, the cankerworm, and the caterpillar, and the palmerworm. . . . And ye shall eat in plenty, and be satisfied, and praise the name of the Lord your God, that hath dealt wondrously with you: and my people shall never be ashamed.

Who but God can judge the value of an individual's life? Who can predict the amount of time it will take to build in the "gold, silver and precious stones" (1 Corinthians 3:12) that comprise a meaningful life?

Remembering once again Raoul Wallenberg and his mission of rescuing Jews, it is important to note that, while he saved the lives of 100,000 Jews in nine months, he languished in Soviet prison camps afterwards—until the present day, if he is still alive. Yet one could say he experienced an active life's work in just those nine months; that is the kind of multiplication of meaning which God can give to a life. The safety zone of meaning can come to one's life in a matter of months or weeks or, perhaps, even in the act of a few seconds.

Managing Your Safety Zones

There are certain times in life which bring out even more effectively than an earthquake that feeling of no foundations, no safety zones. The death of a spouse, a serious illness in a loved one, and certainly illness in one's own body are times which threaten the very foundations of our lives. It is during such times that we are most likely to give up and feel that we must get rid of things or that we can't bear that place where we spent so many happy years with a loved one. Yet given the healing potential of time and the wisdom of knowing how to deal with memories, tasks which overwhelm in a time of grief and places which sear us with the pain of memories can turn into safety zones of comfort.

Safety zones do not remain static. A house which has so many memories of lost loved ones may be too painful to bear in the immediate period following a death. Yet with the passage of time that place of stabbing memories may turn into a safety zone of comfort. Before I lost my family, we used to meet frequently at a certain restaurant. In those days I found that restaurant a little boring. It had no particular negative or positive value for me. After the deaths, however, I did not even want to go near that restaurant. The acute losses seemed amplified by the thought of that place. It played old tapes of loss in me. A few years later I went to a convention in the town where this restaurant is located. At the end of the day, when a friend and I were debating about where to eat, I had a sudden impulse to go back to that restaurant. As I walked inside it felt kind of strange. Even the tables and chairs were still in the same old places. I half expected to see a table with my parents and my aunts and uncles waiting for me. It was a little eerie. But superseding any pain was a feeling of warmth and a flood of happy memories. I don't go there often, because of its distant location, but every once in a while I do go back, just to remember happy times from the past and to feel the warmth of those memories. The restaurant is not spectacular in itself, but to me it has become a safety zone. It has become one of my "places." A place that once I took for granted turned first into a place of pain and then became a very special safety zone.

Remembering that we need change, but that we also need the comfort and security of the old and familiar, it is wise to make *caution* a principle of aging. Don't get rid of things on impulse or in times of discouragement. Wait. Let time heal. Let the earth settle again under your feet, then make those decisions. And don't be overinfluenced by well-meaning people who are different than you or who may not have experienced what you are going through. You, and you alone, can find those things and places which for you provide safety zones of comfort.

For not only do we change in relationship to our safety zones, such as my family restaurant, but sometimes the safety zone itself changes. Another restaurant has always provided a place for me where I can think, talk, and relax. Colleagues and I have met there to exchange ideas. I have celebrated the publication of several books in this place. Even the staff have been part of making this particular place a safety zone for me. In recent months, however, the restaurant has undergone drastic

changes. Some of the staff have left, and
the physical decor has been changed in a
way which makes it feel cold and bleak. The
food has become overly spiced and rich,
and the prices have become nearly prohibi-
tive. Knowing my own resistance to change
I have gone back a few times, just to be
sure. But last week when I rushed through
a meal in order to leave, I knew that this
place was no longer a safety zone for me.

There are times, however, when we feel
as if we are losing a safety zone because we
ourselves have not handled it in a way
which preserves its value to us. Sometimes
we do this by trying to make the safety zone
a place of permanent retreat, rather than
what it should be, a temporary place of ref-
uge. Sometimes we just overuse it, and
safety zones, if they are to last, cannot be
overused.

Christmas has always been a safety
zone to me. I enjoy all the traditions and
memories as well as the present friend-
ships and meaning which I have connected
with it. To me one highlight is my Christmas tree. I have ornaments from my trav-
els, ornaments from my childhood, and ornaments from cherished friends. And each
year a few new ornaments seem to creep
into my growing collection. I used to just
have a pretty tree. But in the last few years
that tree has become bigger and more
elaborate, and people have begun to surprise me by making innocent remarks

about my unique ornaments or how many ornaments there are. They ask other people, "Have you ever seen her tree?"

I used to always play Handel's *Messiah* while decorating the tree. That time was a safety zone every year of enjoying God and worshiping him through the words of that remarkable piece of music. But in the last couple of years I have been too tired to worry about music while I'm doing my tree. Besides, it would take many renditions of that work before the tree would be decorated! I don't do it alone any more either; that, too, would take too long. I have ruined the wonderful safety zone of decorating the Christmas tree by making the end product too elaborate. What was a safety zone has become a chore, even something I dread. The focus of decorating the tree is no longer my own personal satisfaction but impressing others, and as such it no longer is a safety zone for me. It has become an overused, or, in this case, even overextended safety zone.

I have a choice. I can decorate a special tree with help from others, using the kind of effort and organization which that takes. To do this would not necessarily be a wrong choice, for increasingly the tree seems to be a blessing to others. Furthermore, enjoyment of the tree *after* it is done can still be a safety zone for me. But the price tag will be the loss of that old safety zone which the process of decorating the tree provided.

Decorating the Christmas tree has not ceased to be a potential safety zone, nor have I changed so that it can no longer provide that enjoyment for me. The problem has been that I have changed the safety zone too much for it to remain a safety zone.

The Ultimate Safety Zone

For those who have lived long, however, safety zones transcend the preservation of places and things. With age comes a rich storehouse of memories or positive tapes which, while they can be more easily cultivated and enjoyed in conjunction with places and things, cannot be taken away by other people or destroyed by any physical catastrophe. These positive tapes, too, are safety zones. Perhaps this is why we intuitively tend to reminisce more as we get older.

And even if at the end of life some of these treasured memories seem to be destroyed by a failing mind, we can say with missionary Amy Carmichael, "What an awakening one who has walked with Him in the twilight must have, when suddenly she awakes in His likeness and the light is shining round her—all shadowy ways forgotten." [2]

The third verse of one of my favorite hymns reads:

Things that once were wild alarms
Cannot now disturb my rest;
Closed in everlasting arms,
Pillowed on the loving breast.
Oh, to lie forever here,
Doubt, and care, and self resign,
While He whispers in my ear—
I am His, and He is mine. [3]

When all our earthly springs run dry, it is God who is our only unfailing safety zone. He cannot be overused, and thus lose his efficacy as a safety zone. He changes not, and so he can never fail to have those qualities which make up a safety zone. And when we change and move away from him, he is still there, waiting for us to come back to that only perfect safety zone which is to be found in him.

In speaking of the threatening alliance formed against his people, God said,

Neither fear ye their fear, nor be afraid. Sanctify the Lord of hosts himself; and let him be your fear, and let him be your dread (Isaiah 8:12,13).

In a very moving commentary on fear, Viktor Frankl describes being released from a Nazi death camp:

The prisoner's reaction to release can be summed up as follows: at first everything seems to him like a lovely dream; he hardly dares to believe it. After all, he has been deceived by beautiful dreams in the past. How often he dreamed of his liberation—dreamed of coming home, embracing his wife, greeting his

friends, sitting down at table and beginning to
tell the story of his experiences, to describe how
he had longed for this moment of reunion, to
say how many times he had dreamed of this
moment, until at last it had become reality.
And then the three blasts of the whistle shrilled
in his ears, the whistle for the morning rising,
and wrenched him out of the dream. How terrible it was to be brought back to harsh reality.
But finally the day dawns when what has been
longed for and dreamed of actually comes true.
But if on the first day of freedom the present
seems like a lovely dream, in time he reaches
the point where the past seems to be nothing
more than a nightmare. When that time comes,
he himself can no longer understand how he
was able to survive the imprisonment. Hence-
forth he enjoys the precious feeling that after all
he has experienced and suffered, there is nothing left in the world that he need fear—except,
perhaps, his God. For a good many men
learned in concentration camp, and as the result of concentration camp, to believe in God
again. 4

"Let him be your fear, and let him be your
dread." "There is nothing left in the world
that he need fear—except, perhaps, his
God." To know no fear except that of God
alone, and to know the depth of his love for
us, is to have the ultimate safety zone.

Chapter Four

When the Earth Shakes

It was a warm, humid morning in late September. After a summer of unseasonable cold, the California weather had turned unseasonably warm. Yet as I settled down in my chair in the living room, I still enjoyed the warm comfort of my morning cup of coffee. As I simultaneously watched the morning news on television and read the front page of the *Los Angeles Times*, the day seemed normal in spite of the heat. The large, green shade trees outside my living room window reinforced my sense of the usual, as did my dog Horace, munching contentedly on his morning milk bone.

Suddenly, breaking into the tranquility of the morning, came the wrenching devastation of an earthquake. I could hear the sound of glass all through my apartment, and the movement of the apartment itself made me feel as if I were high above the earth on stilts which were ready to give way at any moment. My foundations were gone. My early morning sense of tranquility had vanished. There was no place to hide.

It never once occurred to me that God had lost control or that he would not choose the outcome which was his best will for me. He was still with me. In my humanness I just hoped that he would choose what I wanted—life and safety! Feeling a little cowardly over my tenacious grasp on life, I remembered the words of an old Scottish preacher who said that, although he didn't fear death, he wasn't looking forward to the process. I not only dreaded the process, but I felt that I had not yet finished my task on this earth!

On not quite so philosophical a level, the earthquake made me feel vulnerable and without physical support. In a hundred small and not-so-small ways I felt as though I had no safety zones. Just the ground shaking under my feet and the sound of things falling all around me was enough to make me feel anchorless. But then there was the safety of friends to think about. Were they all okay? How were my patients reacting? Where was my cat? (He had actually been wise enough to hide in a safe place!) And while all these thoughts were rushing through my mind, I could hear the crashing of dishes, vases, and prized possessions—now turned into

pieces of broken debris, to be swept up later
and thrown away. In a few seconds my
tranquil world had been disrupted. My
safety zones, while not annihilated, had
definitely been tampered with.

Many of the negative things which happen to us in life happen slowly. The onset of
certain neuromuscular diseases are so
subtle that the diagnosis may be slow in
coming. The small increase of expenses
which gradually overcome the fixed in-
come, the Christmas cookies which get
harder and harder to make each year, the
slow but steady loss of our friends to illness
and death: these occur with barely percep-
tible speed at first, until suddenly one day
we really notice.

But sometimes our lives are shaken up
abruptly, with the force of a major earthquake. A grandchild is killed on the way to
school. A heart attack strikes when there
have been no prior symptoms. A house
burns down when the family is away on vacation. And whether such disasters come
quietly or crash loudly through the still-
ness of ordinary life, the potential for disas-
ter does seem to be a very real liability of
growing old.

We may find ourselves echoing the words
of Bill Cosby in his book, *Time Flies*:

> Being fifty has an unreality for me. For exam-
> ple, on a television commercial, I hear my friend
> Ed McMahon talking about life insurance that

older people can get and I think, *It's nice that older people can get life insurance.* But suddenly I realize that Ed is talking about *me.* . . .

Am I really that old? Am I really that close to falling down, breaking my hip, and checking out? What a shock it was to be struck by this thought! No matter how many years have passed since I was a boy, I am *still* that boy and I will never be able to see myself as being old enough to break my hip in a fall, . . . At fifty, I know the way of all flesh intellectually, but a part of me still feels as immortal as a child. [1]

The truth is that as we get older there are different, and at times greater, liabilities and assets to face than those that confronted us in the first half of life. Indeed, as time goes on, sometimes the earth beneath us shakes very hard.

When Your "Earthly House" Shakes

As I have talked to various people about their feelings regarding the second half of life, the most predominant fear seems to be that of increased helplessness. We are afraid that as we age we will lose control, that we will be at the mercy of others.

Probably the greatest source of helplessness as we grow older lies in the limitations of our physical being. The body fails. Wrinkles and spots make us feel unlovable. The diminishing of energy often keeps us from doing all that we wish to do. Bones are more brittle, even if we have exercised and taken our calcium pills. And actual disease may strike at a time when we are less resistant to its attack and possess less recuperative powers.

Because of such vulnerabilities, I have heard elderly people make statements like, "I should give this ring to you; my hands aren't pretty anymore." Or they say, "I just can't do things like I used to, so I just won't bother with Christmas this year." Or they back off from social life, declaring, "Those young people won't miss me. I'm no fun at my age." And the list could go on—all denigrations of age itself, as well as of the aging body which has so long served both the individual himself, and the Lord.

As a college student I went through a period of disdain for the physical body. I regarded most funerals, particularly those with open caskets, as being pagan. I rather stoically believed that to push the physical body in serving God, even if that meant physical burn out, was a noble thing to do. Then one Sunday afternoon, as I was expounding on these thoughts, an uncle with whom I was very close said abruptly, "You sound almost gnostic."

Remembering that Gnosticism was the heresy which had infiltrated the church at Colosse, I was a little horrified. But as I thought about it, I realized that my uncle had a point. In most respects nothing I believed related even remotely to gnostic belief, but the Gnostics did have a sense of utter contempt for the human body, which was in direct contradiction to the Christian view of the body as the temple of the Holy Spirit. I had been guilty of going too far in my emphasis on the emotional and spiritual aspects of the human personality, as though they could function on earth without the vehicle of the physical body.

Years later as I stood by the open grave of my mother at the end of the grave-side service, I thought with great warmth of how precious those human remains were. Precious enough to God that some day they will be resurrected once again in a heavenly state of perfection—precious enough that I relinquished them to the earth, even for just a time, with a deep pang of grief.

None of us likes wrinkles and dry skin. None of us wants to be physically weak. But we will certainly age more gracefully if we don't allow ourselves to develop an attitude of disdain for the physical body. After all, as far as cosmetic appearance goes, we can't help what we are born with, but an old face with smile lines and a look of inner contentment is something of which many elderly people can be proud. Such a face is the reflection of the life which has been lived. Conversely, a face which reflects discontent is also the product of the life which has been lived.

Actual physical disability is harder to bear. But it, too, can be handled with more grace if we keep in mind that nothing happens to us that God does not allow. Two biblical principles have been especially helpful in forming my own view of suffering. First, the Bible teaches that God is no man's debtor. No matter what God allows us to suffer, he is never in our debt. He always gives us more than we deserve, not less. He gives much more than he takes. Second, the Bible says that the God of all the earth will do right (Genesis 18:25). Or, in the words of John Byrom:

> With peaceful mind thy race of duty run;
> God nothing does, or suffers to be done,
> But what thou wouldst thy self, if thou
>   couldst see
> Through all events of things as well as
>   He. 2

One of the hardest aspects of physical disability is the resultant dependence, for very often old age brings a partial or even complete role reversal between children and their parents. The loss of support which adult children then feel is disorienting, and can provoke guilt as they realize how much they have taken over their parent's life. The effect on the aging parent is even more difficult, as they sense the loss of control over their own lives.

It is important for all of us as we age to maintain our independence for as long as we can. For many the aging process will never include a complete abdication of

power over their own lives. But even if total
dependence does eventually come, it is best
for all concerned for the elderly person to
control his or her own life for as long as possible. For example, handle your own check
book—forever, if possible. Don't hand it
over to someone else unless your forgetful-
ness is creating too many mistakes. Hand
it over *only* when to do so is in *your* best interest. For in the handling of one's own
money one retains a certain level of independence, regardless of increasing physical dependence.

Your Will Is *Your* Will

Consistent with financial independence
is the planning of what to do with one's
money after death. Whether a person is
twenty or eighty, making a will does not
make you die any more than not making a
will insures that you will live. It simply insures that after your death your money
goes where you want it to go. Such knowledge helps guard against the feeling of loss
of control.

A will is *your* will. It should reflect what
you want, not what your family dictates. It
should be prayerfully decided upon, with
the primary consideration being the will of
God. As Christians our stewardship of
earthly belongings should transcend petty
family quarrels. People who automatically
leave all their material goods to their chil-

dren may or may not be doing the will of God. For that matter, neither is it automatically God's will to simply "leave it to the church." And we can be quite sure that "revenge wills," which leave it all to the family cat, are not motivated by a desire to be a good steward for Jesus Christ.

If a will is contrary to the expectations of the family, or contrary to what is usually done, an accompanying letter can prevent years of fighting between relatives. Because my aunt Lydia stayed home to take care of her, my grandmother left the family farm to her alone. As it turned out, when my aunt sold the farm later on she divided the proceeds with her brother and sisters. But she was under no obligation to do so. In a letter which accompanied the will, addressed to Aunt Lydia, my grandmother wrote with great wisdom about why she was giving her the farm:

> This is intended as an outright gift to you, without any restrictions whatever on your ownership. . . . Not for the purpose of restricting or limiting your ownership of the property in any way, but merely so that you can understand what I have in mind, I would say that, should other members of the family need assistance, it would be my expectation that you would help them, if you were able to do so, out of the income from the farm or proceeds of its sale.

Toward the end of the letter, in anticipation of any objections which the rest of the family might have, she wrote:

> Should any of the members of the family try to interfere with your ownership of the farm, to insist on offering suggestions and advice after you have expressed a desire that they cease to do so, or should any members of the family try to get you to give them an interest in the farm or in the proceeds of its sale, and persist in asking this beyond what you think is fair, it is my desire that you should take this conduct into consideration and, if you think best, decline to do anything whatever for those who have acted in this way.

She concluded:

> I am giving you this farm in the fullest confidence that whatever you may decide upon will be right, and it is my desire that, while the other members of the family are of course free to talk things over with you in a friendly manner, none of them shall try to coerce you or influence your own free judgment.

That will was the will of my grandmother's choosing. It was quite apparent that no one had forced their own "will" upon her. Nonetheless, her accompanying letter wisely protected my aunt Lydia from the possible criticism of others, while it also freed her of any possible feelings of guilt as she pursued God's leading in her use of the inheritance.

I hear children of elderly people speak of their parents' property as "my legacy." Or they complain, "Mother can't buy that. After all, that's our money." Some are shameless enough to declare, "We can't run up that kind of medical expense for Father. That would use up all his money and there would be nothing left for us!" The money and belongings of the elderly are theirs. Until their death they can use it, give it away, burn it if they so desire (although that would certainly not reflect very good stewardship!). And when they make out their will, it should be just that—their final will, not the will of their family or any one else except God alone.

Fearing Dependence

Perhaps even more important than financial independence, although at times related, is physical independence. In spite of severe osteoporosis my aunt Lydia walked several miles a day until she was in her eighties. Rather than let anyone grocery shop for her, she walked to the little corner store and carried her groceries home in small packages. Maybe she went a little far with her independence, but in spite of breaking her hip three times she never stopped being able to walk. She was never required to stay in a convalescent home, beyond the temporary stays after her surgeries. She was never totally dependent.

My mother lived in her own house until she died. In spite of severe arthritis and damaged knee cartilage, she still did the light work in her large garden and took care of her two dogs—this in addition to cooking and housework. That was the way she wanted it and she had the right to choose her own way. Of course she got help from all of us, but the help was given only when she wanted it, and always on her own terms. That is the kind of independence which helps guard against the fear of helplessness in old age.

The idea of helplessness in old age is frightening, particularly because the future is so unknown. "What will happen?" and "How will I handle it?" are questions we all ask, from the first time we realize that we will, in truth, become old someday. When advancing age begins to shake the foundations of our lives, and we find ourselves experiencing things we always hoped would "never happen to us," we'll find that our greatest comfort will be knowing the sovereignty of God.

My parents had two daughters. Several of my aunts and uncles were married and at least had their spouses to depend on. In contrast, my aunt Lydia not only never married but, as it turned out, was the last one of the brothers and sisters to die. She was the proverbial "last leaf." She was therefore the least likely of all her family to be taken care of in her old age. Yet when she began to need a place to live and someone to care for her, I was for the first time in my life in a position to provide that help. And so she always lived at home, with all the care and love she needed until her last hospitalization thirty-six hours before her death. God planned events in his time. His will was sovereign above the fears and apprehensions of man. What looked impossible became possible because it was the will of God. In Matthew 10:29-31 (Weymouth), we read:

> Do not two sparrows sell for a halfpenny? Yet not one of them falls to the ground without your Father's leave. But as for you, the very hairs on your heads are all numbered. Away then with fear; you are more precious than a multitude of sparrows.

Whatever suffering old age may bring, not only is God sovereign but he is also loving.

Sometimes it is hard to give all that we cherish into God's hand for him to take and deal with as he desires. But it is indeed the only safe thing to do. For God "knoweth our frame" and "remembereth that we are dust" (Ps. 103:14). If we cannot imagine a loving earthly father crushing a cherished toy brought to him by his child, neither should we imagine that our heavenly Father will hurt us as we give everything to him. Occasionally a toy is manufactured and then taken off of the market because it is dangerous. Sometimes, too, our "toys"—those things we cherish—are taken away from us by God because we do not see their danger; or they are taken for some other equally valid reason which we may never understand while we are on this earth. But they are taken in love by a Father who loves us forever.

Preparing to Meet the King

Ultimately, the last fear of old age is death itself. For as much as we may long to see the face of our Savior, the process of getting there can be frightening. Even heaven is new, and new is always a little scary. We hear much today about people living on the street in filth, starvation and freezing weather. Yet many of these people refuse shelters, because the fear of the unknown, even though it may be infinitely better than the known, is still frightening since it is unknown. In the same way, when we enter heaven I am sure we will be amazed at the tenacious hold we had on earth, when there was all that glory awaiting us. For as beautiful as this earth can sometimes be—and I, for one, want to stay here as long as I can—"eye hath not seen, nor ear heard, neither have entered into the heart of man, the things which God hath prepared for them that love him" (1 Cor. 2:9).

Not long ago I had the privilege of attending a dinner honoring the king and queen of Sweden. "What shall I wear?" was the question foremost in my mind. It was incredible how long it took to put all the right clothes, jewelry, and accessories together.

Then it took still more time to look up the protocol for meeting royalty. Dining with a king and queen was, in short, an event which required hours of preparation. As I looked back on the event, I could not help but conclude that, if we put such pains into our preparation for meeting an earthly monarch, how much more should we prepare before going into the presence of our heavenly King!

Old age is perhaps granted to some as a time of extra preparation for that moment when we shall become a part of that great cloud of witnesses of Hebrews 12:1. Not long ago I was talking to a retired pastor who had gone through a year of two heart attacks and bypass surgery. "I'm so grateful to God for this period of time which he has given me," he said, "this extra piece of life to become right before him, to purge myself of selfishness, to become more like him before I go to be with him."

My therapist's mind started to contradict him, to tell him he was being way too hard on himself, to make him feel good about himself. Then, as I saw the joy on his face I stopped. For I realized that between his heart and God a very sacred process was going on. A special, final refinement was taking place with which I did not dare to interfere.

Sometimes God gives us a special chance to re-evaluate our lives, to prepare for eternity—not only in the sense of eternal destiny but also in light of our eternal reward. A desire to have eternal reward is not wrong, if it is kept in perspective and not grabbed at greedily. Above all, sometimes God lets his child prepare in a special way for entrance into his divine presence because that child loves his heavenly Father enough to desire to come before him reverently and with great worship.

Growing old is a divine blessing from God, even though the liabilities can at times be severe. For if the liabilities are great, the assets can be even greater. And in spite of all the liabilities, we dare not complain too much—for, quite obviously, the only alternative to growing old is dying young.

Chapter Five

The Best Is Yet to Be

When asked if he would like to be young again, an elderly man replied, "And go through all that? No, thanks." In answer to a similar question another man said, "If I had known how awful old age was going to be, I might have had second thoughts about going through it."

Ask anyone, young or old, about the comparative joys of age versus those of youth, and you will probably find, as I did, that the answers are as unique as the people you ask. Yet most people will be so immersed in their own particular age category that they will find it hard to honestly project themselves into any other age group. The proverbial "other pasture" will always seem greener. The older person will speak of rheumatism or the problems of medicare, and the younger person will complain of unfairness in the marketplace or of the stresses of overwork. Few will be satisfied.

An eleven-year-old summed up the nature of this universal discontent when she said, "When it's something I want, they say I'm too young; when it's something they want, I'm always old enough." In one way or another, most of us feel that way about ourselves in every period of our lives. We fail to echo the words of Paul when he said,

> I indeed have learned, whatever be my outward experiences, to be content. I know both how to live in straitened circumstances and how to live amid abundance. I am fully initiated into all the secrets both of fulness and of hunger, of abundance and of want. I have strength for anything through Him who gives me power (Phil. 4:11-13 Weymouth).

Not long ago I was engaging in the sometimes trivial chitchat which seems to go along with having one's hair done. In a moment of seriousness, I turned to my hairdresser and asked, "What do you think is the greatest asset of growing old?" His answer was that *meaning* was the greatest asset—or, as he applied it to his own case, "knowing that your children turned out okay." As I have asked myself the same question, and then have questioned others in every age group and walk of life, the answer seems the same. What we value most is knowing that we have not lived in vain. We need to feel that our life has had value. We need meaning.

Meaning: God's Will for Each of Us

The whole concept of meaning seems at first glance to be so simple, and yet it increases with complexity as it is focused on. Even the Christian must ask, "What is the *specific* meaning of my life?" As those redeemed by the blood of Christ, we know that we are God's creation, made in his image for fellowship with him. But while the Bible speaks of God's desire for our worship and praise, and for our good works which manifest the reality of the faith within us, it leaves the specific interpretation of how those principles relate to any given life up to the individual. We must each find our meaning by the leading of the Holy Spirit within us.

When I was about twenty-two a friend who was a year younger died. Shortly before dying she said, "I wish I could have lived longer, so that I could have served God more." Her statement expresses something of why we always feel that the death of a young person is so tragic. In our day the term *tragedy* is sometimes used to describe relatively trivial occurrences. During the time of Shakespeare and other Elizabethan writers, tragedy was uniquely defined as the loss of something of great worth. Because of the value of my friend's life as she lived on this earth, from a human point of view her death was truly a tragedy in the Elizabethan sense of that word. The world had lost someone of great worth.

But God doesn't always view worth the way we do. We feel that the longer the life, the greater the worth of that life. To God, however, my friend's life had already completed its purpose on this earth. She was all that he wanted her to be before he took her. From a secular point of view, her death was a tragedy. From God's point of view, her death was in his time.

In God's timetable the specific meaning of any one person's life is not measured in years, or in public acclaim, or in a large bank account. The meaning of life is determined by how much we have lived in the center of God's will for our lives.

I once received a letter from a monk who was just about to take his final vows, including a vow of silence. In his letter he spoke of the Scriptures in a way which indicated his personal knowledge of God. When he told me of the help he had received from one of my books and then promised to pray for my writing, I felt that God had given me the gift of prayer from someone who would obviously have a great deal of time for it. I also imagined that, although he does not share in the "publicness" of writing books, he might indeed share greatly in the eternal reward for any help which people might receive from the books for which he prays. This is probably part of what the Bible means when it says that many we view as first shall be last and many we view as last, shall be first.

It is the uniqueness of God's will for each of our lives which, along with the clarity of biblical precept on this subject, makes me so opposed to euthanasia. I don't relish the prospect of a painful, drawn out terminal illness any more than anyone else. Nor do I believe in extending the dying process by artificial means. But it has not been given to man to choose his date of death, whether he tries to extend it beyond God's time, or whether he terminates it according to his own desired timetable. For part of the meaning of any of our lives may be found in how we die. Who knows what intimate worship may transpire between a person and God in those last hours? Who can speculate on those last days of preparation for entering into the very presence of God Almighty? Our dying, as well as our living, has meaning for God.

As we talk about meaning in life, whether in terms of how we live or how we die, I am compelled to refer once again to 2 Corinthians 3:18, which to me sums up most clearly the biblical view of meaning. W. J. Conybeare's translation reads:

> We all, while with face unveiled we behold in a mirror the glory of the Lord, are ourselves transformed continually into the same likeness; and the glory which shines upon us is reflected by us, even as it proceeds from the Lord, the Spirit. [1]

Bishop Moule states:

A servant of Christ in the past, Lucius von Machtholf, was a man singularly rich in the gift of spiritual influence over individuals. When asked to disclose something of his secret he replied, "I know no other tactics than first of all to be heartily satisfied with my God, even if He should favour me with no sensible visible blessing in my vocation. It were better to be sick in a tent under a burning sun, and Jesus sitting at the tent door, than to be enchanting a thousand listeners where Jesus was not. Never let your inner life get low in your search for the lives of others." His reply, in essence, was that the secret lay, as far as he knew, in the sense of profound contentment with his blessed Master in which his soul was kept through grace. Jesus Christ irradiated him within and for himself. 2

Bishop Moule continues:

The source and the secret was Jesus Christ; and that secret acted equally whether marked success attended speech and action, or apparently no success at all; whether the servant was put by the Master into the front ranks of active reapers in the harvest field, or told to sit down in a corner and sharpen the sickles of others; whether he was called to speak in spiritual power to a multitude, or to lie still on a sick bed. 3

To so settle down in the will of God is the source of truest meaning for the believer in Christ.

Meaningful Use of Time

Meaning in the Christian life is not, however, entirely a private matter between the
believer and God. True faith issues forth
into good works. For retired people this
often means utilizing for the good of others
a resource they have in abundance: *time*.
Indeed, one of the problems of aging is retirement before one is ready—too much
time and too little to do.

When I was working with teenage drug
users a few years ago, I was struck with the
close relationships which young people
often had with their grandparents. They
were very often closer to them than to their
own parents, with whom they often seemed
to be at war. Then I discovered the reason.
So often in our society, age and youth feel
displaced. In years gone by, children were
needed. They helped run the farm or they
worked in the family business. They
churned butter; they made preserves during harvest time; they helped bake the
weekly supply of bread. They were needed.
Now, until they grow up, children are often
a tax deduction at best. They are wanted
and loved, but they are not needed in any
literal sense of that word.

In previous generations, families were
not as mobile as they are today. They
tended to live close to each other, and the
elderly functioned in many practical ways,
ranging from family advisor to cook, baby-

sitter and gardener. They, like their grand-children, were needed.

If aging is to become once again a time of value and productivity, a time which holds meaning for the elderly, then those who re-tire are going to have to take seriously the fact that they still have something to offer. If they don't, no one else will. We don't need to give up and go to a retirement home. Who wants to live with just their own age group anyway. Can you imagine living only with those who are fifty when you are fifty? Or thirty when you are thirty? A variety of life experiences offers opportunity for growth. From the young I remember dreams and keep my idealism. From the old I learn wisdom. From those who are my own age I am reinforced in solving the prob-lems which are peculiar to that age, and I find out that I am not alone.

Cruises and spas are fine for those who are retired. After all, as one gets older see-ing the world and making visits to friends and family who live far away should be part of the reward for all those years of hard work. But a life of full-time entertainment and fun wears thin for most of us, at any age. The years of retirement, where one does not have to worry so much about earn-ing a living, are a legacy from the Lord. They are an opportunity for finding mean-ing. They are extra years to do those good works for which we have never before had time. They are a sacred trust from God.

They offer a second chance to put our faith "into shoeleather."

I know retired people who do valuable volunteer work in hospitals. Some, for example, help by holding babies who have been kept in the hospital following birth. (Every year there are more such babies, as medical technology advances.) Others read to sick children or encourage the terminally ill. Feeding the homeless, chauffeuring the handicapped, doing menial but necessary tasks in a local church: these are just a sample of the myriad of tasks which need doing, and which those who are retired might have the time and inclination to do.

In Numbers 8:25,26 Moses says:

> From the age of fifty years they shall cease waiting upon the service thereof, and shall serve no more: but shall minister with their brethren . . . to keep the charge. . . .

"To keep the charge"—perhaps that is the ultimate work of old age. Commentator C.A. Coates explains:

> When arduous labour is no longer permitted to the Levite he retains an honourable place of ministry with his brethren, and keeps the charge. He is not degraded but rather dignified. . . . He is not dismissed as of no value; . . . he is regarded as one who cherishes all the interests of the service in a peculiar way, for he is to "keep the charge." 4

Above All, Time to Pray

For those who are handicapped by the frailties which can accompany the aging process, an encouraging note or phone call to someone who needs hope is another type of ministry which can still be done. And above all, perhaps the elderly have more time than ever in their lives before to really pray.

Not long ago a woman said to me, "I'm so tired that all I can do is pray. At least that doesn't take any energy."

In amazement I responded, "Prayer is work. If you expect to rest, don't try intercessory prayer!"

Prayer is work. But it is work which truly builds in the "gold, silver, precious stones" of 1 Corinthians 3:12. Prayer takes time. And time is what many of us will have more of as we get older. Prayer is an unseen ministry which will reap most of its reward only in eternity. But what a reward that will be! Many of the elderly and the handicapped will suddenly be very prominent when they reach heaven, because of their unseen prayers for great works of God on this earth. There can be few ministries on this earth which exceed the greatness of a ministry of prayer; and who are more qualified to perform this ministry than those who have the balance and perspective of experience and the time which usually accompanies retirement?

Someone has said that the only people who fear death are those who have never lived. The same might also be said of aging. If our life has lacked meaning, we will fear old age—for it will indicate to us that our life is nearing an end while we have not yet really lived.

Ultimately, the full meaning of our lives will be completed only in heaven, when we are in God's presence. As Conybeare's translation of 1 Corinthians 13:12 reads:

> So, now we see darkly, by a mirror, but then face to face; now I know in part, but then shall I know, even as I now am known. . . . 5

Yet a very challenging aspect of the Christian life is that it is a preparation for the life to come. After salvation, this earth is where we Christians grow. It is our place of refining, where we gradually change into his image. The Bible is clear that we never reach absolute perfection on earth. But the refining process should be complete enough that when we go into his presence the change will not be that drastic.

In counseling people who are depressed, I have noticed that sometimes people who wish to die will change their minds when they realize they have been placed on earth for a specific purpose and with unique timing. It is awesome to realize that, when you tamper with the duration of a human life, whether that life is your own or someone else's, you are taking into your own hands

God's purposes for that life. You are tampering with your own or another person's eternal reward. Often this realization in itself will prevent a person from ending their life as well as give them a meaning for their life which will preclude any future desire for suicide.

Long life is a gift from God. It offers that valuable gift of time in which to fulfill the will of God. It offers opportunity for meaning. For while God is not limited by time as we know it, in order to fulfill his will in us he does seem to give some people extra time to do and become more for him. This is one of the blessings of long life. The storehouses are full of deeds done for God as well as worship offered up to him. For old age has a past which cannot be taken away. Youth, on the other hand, has its promise of life primarily in the uncertain future.

Riches Unenjoyed

There are many people who have their storehouses full who cannot enjoy that knowledge in their later years. Because of their innate self-distrust they never realize the meaning which their lives have had. They never benefit from growing older.

The middle-aged pastor of a small church called me in a state of considerable discouragement. I know for a fact that this man does a deep work for God. He has a close relationship with God, and many people in the community are helped by his counsel and practical deeds of kindness. Yet as he told me that afternoon of the encouragement he had received from reading about the lives of great Christians, he concluded drearily, "They helped me so much until I remembered that I'm not like them. I'm not the great saint that any of them were. So how can I expect God to work in my life as he did in theirs?" This man doesn't believe God could really care about him because he doesn't care about himself. He doesn't take himself seriously enough to see and enjoy the meaning which his life possesses.

The concept of self-esteem is badly misunderstood in our culture. Yet many people are hindered in their Christian life, rather than helped as some might think, by a chronically low self-image. A person's self-image needs to be based on truth. The positive aspects of one's personality can then be cultivated and enjoyed, while those qualities which are negative can be improved upon. A good self-image is not the result of psychiatric manipulation; it must be based on truth if it is to prove worthwhile.

Kenneth Wuest translates Romans 12:3:

> For I am saying through the grace which is given to everyone who is among you, not to be thinking more highly of one's self, beyond that which one ought necessarily to be thinking, but to be thinking with a view to a sensible ap-

praisal (of one's self) according as to each one
God divided a measure of faith. 6

Wuest then comments that a person is
"'to think' that is, appraise his gifts rightly,
but not become proud of them." 7

Pride does not reflect a good self-image.
Conversely, my pastor-friend who dislikes
himself so much is not displaying humility.
He just doesn't like himself. And in the
same way, another pastor who communi-
cates to everyone that he is the prince of all
pastors is most likely also suffering from a
low self-image. He really doesn't like himself at all or he wouldn't have to try so hard
to convince everyone, himself included,
that he is truly okay. Pride and false humility are usually manifestations of the same
root problem: a low self-image. To avoid
self-aggrandizement in general, or to be
able to work with equal grace in the back-
ground or the foreground: that is humility.
The best manifestation of humility is a simple self-forgetfulness, but there is a vast
difference between self-forgetfulness and
self-denigration.

The kind of self-esteem mentioned in Romans is far different from that which is
taught by even some who call themselves
Christians. A humanistic self-worship, or
a love of self which is based on untruth, or a
focus on self which is an end in itself, are all
distortions of that sense of self-acceptance
which is God-given. If I cook well, or play

the piano well, or just have pretty eyes, can it be godly to deny these assets as though these God-given good qualities were worthless? Does it make sense that God made us in his image only to demand that we hate this contemptible creation as something he must have made in an off moment?

Again, we humans tend to go to such extremes. We hate ourselves or we worship ourselves. We deny that mankind has some pretty good qualities because we see qualities in some which are not so nice. We confuse sin with humanness. We equate the old nature of Romans 6 with an acceptance of ourselves, which has nothing to do with the self or the sin nature of the Scriptures, but refers to the personality, talents and sense of character which God has given to each of us and has helped us to develop for him. We forget that when we compare ourselves with God, we are nothing. But at the same time, in our comparisons with each other we will have both weak and strong points. I may swim better than my neighbor, but she may be more proficient in tennis.

Missionary Unaware

When my aunt Lydia was a young girl, her dream was to be a missionary in South America. Then her father and older sister died within a few years of each other, my aunt Ruth went to China, my mother and

uncle both got married and my aunt Lydia
decided that what God was asking her to do
was to take care of her elderly mother. She
never got to South America. But after her
mother died she did take care of Ruth, who
had come home from China with malnutri-
tion. And later still she took care of my uncle, who was considerably older. She
stayed home and took care of things so that
others could do their works for God.

As my aunt Lydia got older she would say
things like, "I never did anything great for
God," or "I wish I could have served God
more." Her life had meaning, but she
couldn't see it to the degree that God
wanted her to see it. She couldn't enjoy the
safety zone of meaning to its fullest because
she doubted the value of what she had
done. She doubted herself. What a surprise it must have been a few years ago
when she heard that "well done" from the
Lord she had served all her days. Her
earthly life was not glamorous or public,
but it had great meaning.

I once saw a teenage boy in my office who
had been badly abused by his natural parents. The abuse had been hidden until Bill
was about ten. Then he was taken from his
parents and, eventually, at the age of twelve
he was adopted by some very caring people.
His self-hate was so great, however, that he
couldn't believe anyone really cared. And
so he tested his new parents and in general
made life miserable for them in his at-

tempts to prove that he was really too terrible to love. After all, hadn't his "real" parents tried to hurt him? "They must have had a reason," his young mind had concluded.

When Bill came into my office the first time I wondered if I would ever reach him. "I hate myself, everyone else hates me, and you're not going to change that!" he declared defiantly. Nor did I, until two sessions later he slipped and let me know that he did believe in God's love.

Quickly I countered, "Do you believe that God makes junk?"

"Of course not," was his comeback, said rather arrogantly, as though he had finally showed me up in all of my stupidity.

"Then how come he made you?" I retorted.

A dead silence filled the room. Bill looked at me and grinned for the first time. "I never thought of that," he said. It took a long time to rebuild a self-image which had been so badly battered. But after that exchange it was possible to begin. To me it was a magnificent manifestation of how biblical Christianity and sound psychology can join in the healing of persons.

God doesn't make junk, and God doesn't waste time. He who counts the hairs on our heads, he who knows about the fall of every sparrow, he is the God who also measures out our days on this earth. We live in his time, and he has a purpose for each day

and each hour. His task is to give us his
chosen life span and the resources for that
life. Our task is to seek out the details of his
plan for our lives and to choose so to live.

A. B. Simpson, pioneer church leader
and hymn writer, wrote the striking lines, "I
take, he undertakes." Sometimes we live
spiritually like those who have great bank
accounts from which to draw and yet never
draw from those accounts. We choose to
live in poverty. Nor do we choose to see
each day as a valuable legacy from God.
Then we wonder why our lives lack meaning.

Old age does not need to be a time of im-
poverishment. It can be a time when the
spiritual granaries are full. And for those
who have not made wise choices, it is consistent with our Lord's love that the second
half can be a time of getting back what the
locusts have eaten. For Scripture shows
clearly that lost time can be made up if we
so choose.

It is important to realize that, for all of us
at any age, only God knows the future and
only God controls that future.

That famous preacher of nineteenth-
century England, Charles H. Spurgeon,
said in one sermon:

> Now, you middle-aged men, you are plunged in
> the midst of business, and are sometimes sup-
> posing what will become of you in your old age.
> But is there any promise of God to you, when
> you suppose about tomorrow? You say, "Sup-

pose I should live to be as old as So-and-so, and
be a burden upon the people, I should not like
that." Don't get meddling with God's business;
leave his decrees to him. There is many a person who thought he would die in a workhouse
that has died in a mansion; and many a woman
that has thought she would die in the streets,
has died in her bed, happy and comfortable,
singing of providential grace and everlasting
mercy. Middle-aged man! Listen to what David
says, again, "I have been young, and now am
old; yet have I not seen the righteous forsaken,
nor his seed begging bread." Go on, then, un-
sheath thy sword once more. "The battle is the
Lord's;" leave thy declining years to him and
give thy present years to him. Live to him now,
and he will never cast you away when you are
old. 8

Mission Accomplished

What it means to have meaning in life will
vary from person to person. But to have a
sense of meaning is essential in aging
gracefully. For through meaning we reap
increasing reward in the second half of life.
Not long before my father's death he turned
to me and said, "You know, everything I set
out to do in this life I have done. I've
reached all my major goals." It was an
amazing statement, for it was not like him
to be so forthright about his inner feelings.
And he only said it once.

Just a few weeks later, as a pastor friend
stood by his bed—just minutes before a
second major stroke took away his power to

speak forever—my father said, "It is the grace of God which has brought me this far. And the grace of God will bring me through." His next words were spoken in the presence of God a few weeks later. He had fought the good fight. He had built up his storehouse of meaning—had known the reward of meaning—on this earth. And then he went to an even greater reward in heaven.

Notes

Chapter One:
1 Handley C. G. Moule, *The Second Epistle to the Corinthians: A Translation, Paraphrase, and Exposition* (Grand Rapids, Michigan: Zondervan, 1962), 24

2 Robert Browning, "Rabbi Ben Ezra"

3 Alan Pifer and Lydia Bronte, eds., *Our Aging Society: Paradox and Promise* (New York: W. W. Norton & Co., 1986), 4

4 Ibid., 11,12

5 Colin M. Turnbull, *The Mountain People* (New York: Simon and Schuster, 1972), 286

6 Ibid., 291

7 Ibid., 294

8 Quoted in William Manchester, *"American Caesar" Douglas MacArthur* (Boston: Little, Brown & Co., 1978), 702

Chapter Two:
1 Viktor E. Frankl, *The Doctor and the Soul* (New York: Vintage Books, 1973), 44

2 Ibid.

3 Ibid.,137

4 F. L. Godet, *Commentary on the First Epistle of St. Paul to the Corinthians* (Grand Rapids, Michigan: Zondervan, 1957), 123

Chapter Three:

1 Viktor E. Frankl, *The Unheard Cry for Meaning* (New York: Simon and Schuster, 1978), 104,105

2 Amy Carmichael, *Candles in the Dark* (Fort Washington, Pennsylvania: Christian Literature Crusade, 1981), 59

3 George Wade Robinson, "Loved With Everlasting Love"

4 Viktor E. Frankl, *The Doctor and the Soul* (ibid.), 103,104

Chapter Four:

1 Bill Cosby, *Time Flies* (New York: Doubleday, 1987), 149,150

2 John Byrom, *Miscellaneous Poems, Vol. 2* (Leeds: Printed by and for James Nichols, 1814) p. 219

Chapter Five:

1 William John Conybeare, *The Epistles of Paul: A Translation and Notes* (Grand Rapids, Michigan: Baker Book House, 1958), 57

2 Handley C. G. Moule, *The Second Epistle to the Corinthians: A Translation, Paraphrase, and Exposition* (Grand Rapids: Zondervan, 1962), 30,31

3 Ibid., 31

4 C. A. Coates, *An Outline of the Book of Numbers* (Great Britain: Purnell and Sons, Ltd.), 110,111

5 William John Conybeare, *The Epistles of Paul: A Translation and Notes* (ibid.), 40

[6] Kenneth Wuest, *Romans in the Greek New Testament* (Grand Rapids, Michigan: William B. Eerdmans, 1955), 211

[7] Ibid., 210

[8] C. H. Spurgeon, quoted in, *The Sermons of Rev. C. H. Spurgeon, Vol. II* (New York: Funk & Wagnall Co., 1892), 378